STRANGER WORLDS
COLORING BOOK

STRANGER WORLDS
COLORING BOOK

JUAN CALLE AND
SANTIAGO CALLE

SIRIUS

SIRIUS

This edition published in 2024 by Sirius Publishing, a division of
Arcturus Publishing Limited,
26/27 Bickels Yard, 151–153 Bermondsey Street,
London SE1 3HA

ISBN: 978-1-3988-4044-7
CH012113NT

Printed in China

INTRODUCTION

Starting with a giant monster from the primeval swamp, dripping with goo and a danger to all comers, the images within will take you from there into an Egyptian tomb to encounter the distorted features of a jackal-headed god and the supposedly bucolic environs of a forest where terrifying creatures lurk within: a skeletal creature with antlers on its skinless scalp, or eyeless things whose bony hands reach out from the dark to grab the unsuspecting.

There are monsters from the deep as well with rising tentacles and worms with many-toothed mouths; massive octopuses who raise their limbs up through the ocean to grab and encircle passing ships; while others summon the dead, such as the bulbous monster controlling a zombie army of medieval knights.

Whatever your predilection, if you're a fan of otherworldly figures, grab your colored pencils, and create your own blood-curdling creation from the outlines on these pages.

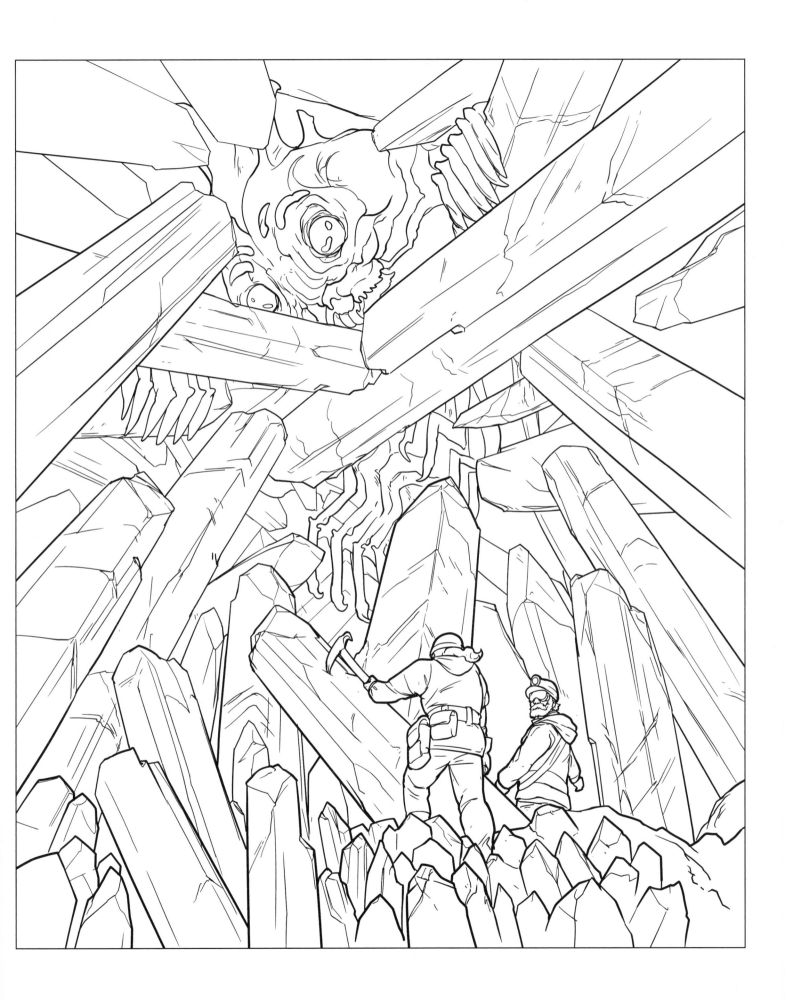